Babe Didrikson Zaharias

Jennifer Strand

abdopublishing.com

Published by Abdo Zoom™, PO Box 398166, Minneapolis, Minnesota 55439. Copyright © 2017 by Abdo Consulting Group, Inc. International copyrights reserved in all countries. No part of this book may be reproduced in any form without written permission from the publisher. Abdo Zoom™ is a trademark and logo of Abdo Consulting Group, Inc.

Printed in the United States of America, North Mankato, Minnesota
072016
092016

Cover Photo: Bettmann/Corbis
Interior Photos: Bettmann/Corbis, 1; AP Images, 4, 5, 9, 11, 16, 17; Lamar University Archives Special Collection, 6, 7, 8; Getty Images, 10; George Rinhart/Corbis/Getty Images, 12; Bettmann/Getty images, 13, 14–15, 18; Ed Mahoney/ AP images, 19

Editor: Emily Temple
Series Designer: Madeline Berger
Art Direction: Dorothy Toth

Publisher's Cataloging-in-Publication Data
Names: Strand, Jennifer, author.
Title: Babe Didrikson Zaharias / by Jennifer Strand.
Description: Minneapolis, MN : Abdo Zoom, [2017] | Series: Trailblazing athletes
    | Includes bibliographical references and index.
Identifiers: LCCN 2016941529 | ISBN 9781680792492 (lib. bdg.) |
    ISBN 9781680794175 (ebook) | 9781680795066 (Read-to-me ebook)
Subjects: LCSH: Zaharias, Babe Didrikson, 1911-1956--Juvenile literature. |
    Athletes--United States--Biography--Juvenile literature. | Women athletes--
    United States--Biography--Juvenile literature.
Classification: DDC 796.0922 [B]--dc23
LC record available at http://lccn.loc.gov/2016941529

Table of Contents

Babe Didrikson Zaharias
was a great **athlete**.

4

She played many sports.
She helped start women's
professional golf.

Babe was born on
June 26, 1911. She grew up
in Texas. Few girls at this
time played sports.

But Babe played many sports well.

She was **competitive**.
Her best sport
was basketball.

Later she became
a track-and-field star.

Rise to Fame

Didrikson made the
US Olympic team in 1932.

She won three medals.
Two were gold medals. She also
broke two world records.

Superstar

Didrikson began
playing golf.

She won a championship
for **amateur** golfers.

Female golfers were uncommon. So she helped make a group to support them.

It was called
the Ladies
Professional Golf
Association.

Didrikson married
George Zaharias.
She continued to win
many golf tournaments.
But she got sick.

She stopped playing in 1955.

Babe Didrikson Zaharias died on September 27, 1956.

Her example inspired many
female athletes.

Babe Didrikson Zaharias

Born: June 26, 1911

Birthplace: Port Arthur, Texas

Husband: George Zaharias

Sports: Basketball, Track and Field, Golf

Known For: Didrikson Zaharias was a star athlete. She helped advance women's sports.

Died: September 27, 1956

1911: Mildred Ella "Babe" Didrikson is born on June 26.

1932: Didrikson wins three medals in track and field at the Olympics.

1934: Didrikson enters her first golf tournament.

1938: Didrikson marries professional wrestler George Zaharias.

1947: Didrikson Zaharias wins the Ladies British Amateur Championship.

1956: Didrikson Zaharias dies on September 27.

Glossary

amateur - someone who does a sport or hobby for fun rather than as a job.

athlete - a person who plays a sport.

competitive - having a strong desire to win.

professional - paid to do something.

record - a statistic, mark, or measurement that is unmatched.

Booklinks

For more information on
Babe Didrikson Zaharias, please visit
booklinks.abdopublishing.com

Z⌕m In on Biographies!

Learn even more with the Abdo Zoom
Biographies database. Check out
abdozoom.com for more information.

Index